THE REFUGEE HOTEL

THE REFUGEE HOTEL

Carmen Aguirre

Talonbooks

Talonbooks
278 East First Avenue, Vancouver, British Columbia, V5T 1A6
www.talonbooks.com

Third printing: January 2018

Typeset in Scala
Printed and bound in Canada on Forest Stewardship Council–certified paper

Cover design by Adam Swica

Talonbooks acknowledges the financial support of the Canada Council for the Arts, the Government of Canada through the Canada Book Fund, and the Province of British Columbia through the British Columbia Arts Council and the Book Publishing Tax Credit.

Rights to produce *The Refugee Hotel*, in whole or in part, in any medium by any group, amateur or professional, are retained by the author. Interested persons are requested to contact Carmen Aguirre care of Talonbooks.

LIBRARY AND ARCHIVES CANADA CATALOGUING IN PUBLICATION

Aguirre, Carmen, 1967–
        The refugee hotel / Carmen Aguirre.
A play.
ISBN 978-0-88922-650-0
        I. Title.
PS8601.G86R44 2010   C812'.6   C2010-902243-2

I return to the South, the way one always returns to love. I return to you, with my desire, with my fear. I carry the South like the destiny of my heart. I am of the South. I dream of the South, immense moon, upside down sky. I search for the South, for the open time and its aftermath. I love the South, its good people, its dignity. I feel the South, like your body in the dark. I love you, South.

—Fernando Pino Solanas

I am grateful to life, which has given me so much: two open eyes that allow me to distinguish the darkness from the light.

—Violeta Parra

They were nothing more than people, by themselves. Even paired, any pairing, they would have been nothing more than people by themselves. But all together, they have become the heart and muscles and mind of something perilous and new, something strange and growing and great. Together, all together, they are the instruments of change. —Keri Hulme

Come with me, along the great avenue, where a new destiny will be born. Come with me, to the heart of the Earth. Friend, bring your child, brother, bring your mother, all of us along the great avenue. The time of the wind has come, exploding the silence.

—Victor Jara

The wind whistles within me.
I am naked. Master of nothing, master of no one, not even master of my own convictions, I am my face in the wind, against the wind, and I am the wind that strikes my face.

—Eduardo Galeano

Love is the answer ... Yes is the answer ... Yes is surrender ...

—John Lennon

I dedicate The Refugee Hotel *to Nelson Rodríguez, because he never forgot.*

To Bob Everton, because he never gave up.

Acknowledgements

I would like to thank the Canada Council for the Arts and the British Columbia Arts Council for individual writing grants. I wrote the first draft of the play during my residency at the Vancouver Playhouse. The Playwrights' Theatre Centre in Vancouver provided a week-long workshop of the second draft and produced a workshop production of said draft. A heartfelt thanks to the 2002 Banff Playrites Colony, where I completed the third draft. The Factory Theatre's Cross Currents Festival (Toronto), The Arts Club Theatre's REACT Festival (Vancouver), and The Mark Taper Forum's New Works Festival (Los Angeles) all held public readings of different drafts of the play. I am grateful to all of them.

I would like to thank Glynis Leyshon, Elizabeth Dancoes, and Pier Carlo Talenti for dramaturgical support in the early drafts of the play. Big gratitude as well to Guillermo Verdecchia for his mentorship and support in the last fifteen years, and for his keen dramaturgical eye and feedback during rehearsals of *The Refugee Hotel*. I am eternally grateful to dramaturg Brian Quirt for all his work on this project.

To the dozens of actors and directors who gave their all to each reading of every draft, eternal gratitude as well.

Above all, I would like to thank Marilo Núñez for her unwavering belief in this play and for seeing it through to its world premiere.

The Refugee Hotel was produced by Alameda Theatre Company in association with Theatre Passe Muraille. It premiered at Theatre Passe Muraille on September 16, 2009, with the following cast and crew:

Manuel: Salvatore Antonio
Male Cueca Dancer: Felix Basáez
Pat Kelemen: Leanna Brodie
Receptionist: Terrence Bryant
Cristina: Cheri Maracle
Isabel: Paloma Núñez
Flaca: Beatriz Pizano
Manuelita: Paula Rivera / Michelle Polak
Juan: Michael Scholar Jr.
Joselito: Osvaldo Sepulveda
Bill O'Neill: Todd Thomson
Fat Jorge: Juan Carlos Velis

Producer: Marilo Núñez
Director: Carmen Aguirre
Dramaturg: Brian Quirt
Set Designer: Trevor Schwellnus
Lighting Designer: Itai Erdal
Costume Designer: Andjelija Djuric
Sound Designer: Nano Valverde
Production Manager: Doug Morum
Stage Manager: Andrea Schurman
Assistant Stage Manager: Wendy Lee
Assistant Director: Alex Castillo
Assistant Producer: Sigrid Velis
Head of Wardrobe: Barbara Rowe

Synopsis

A dark comedy about a group of Chilean refugees who arrived in Vancouver in 1974 and were put up in a modest hotel. An uncompromising look at exile, torture, guilt, and betrayal, *The Refugee Hotel* is ultimately about love and its power to heal.

Cast of Characters

MANUELITA, adult in the present, eight in the past.

JOSELITO, ten.

FAT JORGE (father of Manuelita and Joselito), thirties.

FLACA (mother of Manuelita and Joselito), thirties.

ISABEL (CALLADITA), early twenties.

CRISTINA (CAKEHEAD), eighteen.

MANUEL (CONDOR PASSES), seventeen.

JUAN (OF THE CHICKENS), early twenties.

BILL O'Neill, mid-twenties.

RECEPTIONIST (Jackie), sixties.

PAT Kelemen (social worker), thirties.

MALE CUECA DANCER (a trickster; the soul of Chile, Chile itself, the dictatorship, memory; Eros. He is woven throughout the script. In production one might find more opportunities to weave him in. The whole cast sees him in the prologue and when the song "El Aparecido" is played. For the rest of the play, Fat Jorge sees him, as does Manuel. The others sense him).

DOCTOR

About the Set

A multi-level set is ideal. When a scene is happening in the lobby or in one of the rooms, the other hotel occupants remain in their rooms, seen by the audience.

The play takes place in Vancouver, over a one-week period in February 1974, five months after the coup in Chile.

Prologue

The stage is dark. We hear the sound of a radio dial being turned. Static, until the radio catches the final phrases of Salvador Allende's last speech, broadcast directly from La Moneda Palace on the morning of the coup. Footage of Allende's popular unity rally is projected onto a banner held by the cast members. The entire cast, except for the CUECA DANCER, stands on stage, witnessing. Once Allende's speech is finished, ADULT MANUELITA translates the broadcast.

ADULT MANUELITA:
I know we are living a bitter moment in Chile's history, but I have faith that much sooner than later the great avenues of this country will open once again, where the free man will build a new society. Long live Chile, long live the people, long live the working class. These are my final words ...

The sound of bombs being dropped on La Moneda Palace, full blast. Footage of the bombing, the coup, and its aftermath. Absolute silence. ADULT MANUELITA remains centre-stage, suitcase in hand. We begin to hear the zapateo of a lone male MALE CUECA DANCER. The DANCER emerges, dressed in full huaso gear. He brings the hotel to life.

ADULT MANUELITA:
(walking around the set, contemplating the hotel) If these walls could speak, they'd tell you a story about the past that informs the present and illuminates the future. It was one week in the month of February. It poured with rain the whole time. It was 1974 and the décor was ... *(Lights start to come up. The MALE CUECA DANCER continues to dance.)* ... red shag carpets, plastic orange light shades, macramé, a bean bag in the corner and—ah, yes—the lava lamp.

It takes courage to remember, it takes courage to forget, it takes a hero to do both.

The CUECA DANCER does a full-on zapateo and exits.

MANUELITA's family (FAT JORGE, FLACA, and JOSELITO), PAT Kelemen, and the RECEPTIONIST remain on stage, creating a tableau: FAT JORGE, FLACA, and JOSELITO carry suitcases. PAT Kelemen leads them, briefcase in hand. The RECEPTIONIST sits behind his desk, talking on the phone. ADULT MANUELITA, suitcase in hand, joins her family.

We are taken back to 1974. MANUELITA is now a child.

The rest of the cast exits.

ACT ONE

Scene One

PAT:
Ici we are.

RECEPTIONIST:
(*into the phone*) You're not listening—

PAT:
Excuse me.

RECEPTIONIST:
(*into the phone*) No. Put the phone to your RIGHT ear.

PAT:
I'm Pat Kelemen.

RECEPTIONIST:
(*into the phone*) Mum?

PAT:
The social worker assigned to the Chilean refugees.

RECEPTIONIST:
(*into the phone*) Your right EAR. (*to SOCIAL WORKER*) Hotel's booked. (*into the phone*) WHAT'S wrong with your clock?

PAT:
I know—

RECEPTIONIST:
(*to SOCIAL WORKER*) Solid. (*into the phone*) Your kidneys are fine, Mum. (*louder*) I said they're fine!

PAT:
This is the González family.

RECEPTIONIST:

(*into the phone*) Listen—

PAT:

The refugees.

RECEPTIONIST:

(*into the phone*) I thought I could take the ferry over for high tea at The Empress—

PAT:

(*to the family*) I'm so sorry about this. (*to the RECEPTIONIST*) Do you speak Spanish?

RECEPTIONIST:

(*into the phone*) I thought you LIKED The Empress.

PAT:

(*to the family*) Ayayayayay.

RECEPTIONIST:

(*into the phone*) Look, Mum? I'm going to have to call you back. (*hanging up the phone*) WHAT is the problem?!

PAT:

I don't know what to do. They don't speak a word of English and all I know is French. (*to the family, speaking very slowly and loudly*) This is it!

RECEPTIONIST:

(*adjusting his spectacles*) THESE are the refugees?

PAT:

Of course they are.

(*to the family*) Ici! Uh ... le hotel! Tu stay ici until moi can place tu in a casa! Comprendez?

FLACA:

Say something, Fat Jorge. Can't you see the woman's talking to us?

FAT JORGE:

Of course I can see that, Flaca! What makes you think I'd understand her?

FLACA:
(*to SOCIAL WORKER*) This is a very nice hotel, so modern.

JOSELITO:
Look, Mom, they have a TV!

FLACA:
Just be quiet now, Joselito. Can't you see your mother's trying to communicate? (*to SOCIAL WORKER, very loudly*) I was saying that this is a nice hotel, but we don't have any money to pay for it!

PAT:
(*to RECEPTIONIST*) Do you understand what she's saying?

RECEPTIONIST:
(*handing her the key, grabbing his newspaper*) Uh-uh. The man needs a good hit of scotch.

FLACA:
The gringo doesn't like us. He's catching on that we have no money. Fat Jorge, tell the woman we can't pay for the hotel, before the old gringo calls the cops on us—

FAT JORGE:
Nobody's calling the cops on us, Flaca.

MANUELITA:
I'm tired.

FLACA:
Just be quiet, Manuelita. Your father and I are trying to figure something out.

PAT:
Well, pourquoi we not go arriba to your room, now, comprendez?

FLACA:
Excuse me, we can't pay for the hotel. We don't have money. But as soon as we find work, we'll pay the bill. I can assure you of that. Maybe we can sign a paper saying that we will pay you for sure. Fat Jorge! Help me out here!

FAT JORGE:

(*to SOCIAL WORKER*) I am a hard-working man and I will pay for the hotel as soon as I get a job! I promise!

FLACA:

Let's give her the ten dollars we have. So she understands.

FAT JORGE:

(*handing SOCIAL WORKER the money*) Here. That's all we have for now. Tomorrow, first thing, I will find a job and pay for the rest.

PAT:

What are you doing? No! No! Keep your—uh—dinero! Le hotel is paid for! Let's go up to your room now! You need to rest! Siesta!—You've had a long flight! I'm sure you're tired. Let's go. Vamos. Arriba.

JOSELITO:

I'm hungry!

MANUELITA:

I have to go pee!

JOSELITO:

And thirsty.

The SOCIAL WORKER starts walking up the stairs.

PAT:

Come on! Let's go! Moi, tu, everybody, arriba.

FLACA:

Okay kids, let's go.

The family follows her up the stairs, carrying their suitcases.

JOSELITO:

This hotel looks just like the TV shows.

FAT JORGE:

How are we going to pay for this? One night here must cost a month's wages.

FLACA:

Don't worry the kids. They have enough on their minds already.

They arrive at the room.

PAT:

Okay. Perfecto. A grande bed and dos chicos. Ici is where tu will sleep, uh, siesta. Zzzzz. You have a kitchenette, comida, and there's a mercado just up the calle for tu to do your groceries. *(handing FLACA some cash)* Ici tu go. This should be enough dinero for the next few dias. *(handing FLACA her card)* Ici is my card. If you have any pourquois, por favor call moi. Mi nombre es Pat. Pat Kelemen. Moi ici to provide any support tu may need. Comprendez?

The SOCIAL WORKER leaves. The family all lie down on the double bed and fall asleep, on top of each other, with their coats still on.

The SOCIAL WORKER walks down the stairs.

PAT:

(to RECEPTIONIST) I think they're in trauma.

RECEPTIONIST:

(not looking up from his newspaper) Did you see her earrings? Solid lapis lazuli hanging down to her shoulders.

Scene Two

Later that night. Everyone has fallen asleep. All the family is sleeping on the double bed, on top of each other. The CUECA DANCER dances in the background. The sound of pan pipes is heard. There is a lone light on the bed.

FAT JORGE is having a flashback/nightmare. There is the sound of weeping, pleading, sniffling. A baby cries. FAT JORGE screams.

FLACA:
(*shaking FAT JORGE*) Fat Jorge! Fat Jorge! Wake up! Wake up!

FAT JORGE jerks up. He stares around the room.

MANUELITA:
The bathroom's over there!

JOSELITO:
Don't throw up on the Canadian bed, Dad!

FAT JORGE runs to the bathroom and pukes. He comes back.

FLACA:
Come over here, my little big bear. It's okay. Everything's going to be okay.

FAT JORGE:
Ow. Don't squeeze my gut. I'm just gonna go downstairs and pace a little bit—

FLACA:
Kids, we're staying here.

FAT JORGE:
—get my heart to slow down.

27

Scene Three

FAT JORGE goes down to the lobby. Gentlemen Prefer Blondes *is on TV. The RECEPTIONIST mouths along to "Diamonds Are a Girl's Best Friend."*

RECEPTIONIST:
(*seeing FAT JORGE*) Oh!

FAT JORGE stares at the RECEPTIONIST.

RECEPTIONIST:
Friday night classics. Channel twelve.

FAT JORGE:
(*nodding*) Jes jes.

They stare at each other for an awkward moment. The RECEPTIONIST goes back to watching TV.

FAT JORGE looks out the window. The sound of pouring rain. He pulls out a small bottle of rum, the kind you get at airport duty-free shops. He takes a swig.

FLACA has made sure the children are asleep and she comes down the stairs. She approaches FAT JORGE.

FLACA:
How you doing?

FAT JORGE:
(*quickly hiding mickey*) It rains hard here.

FLACA:
Yeah.

Long pause as they both contemplate the rain out the window.

FLACA:

You've lost a lot of weight, Fat Jorge.

FAT JORGE:

Well, the meals weren't great.

FLACA:

My little big bear.

FAT JORGE:

My Mona Lisa.

Pause.

FLACA:

It was so surreal being on that plane after not seeing you and the kids for so long and not really being able to talk.

FAT JORGE:

We talked.

FLACA:

I mean about the real stuff.

FAT JORGE:

Yeah. My ears were plugged half the time anyway, so I wouldn't have been able to hear you. There. I made you laugh. At least I still make you laugh. Remember our first date? September 21, 1962. The first day of spring. I took you dancing and did the twist and put my back out and you peed yourself laughing.

FLACA:

That's when I knew you were the one.

FAT JORGE:

But really. Nobody ever told me that your ears plug on planes.

FLACA:

Or that you fly right through the clouds.

Pause.

FAT JORGE:

It rains really, really hard here.

FLACA:

I'm sorry.

FAT JORGE:
What are you sorry about?

FLACA:
About what happened.

FAT JORGE:
What happened?

FLACA:
Fat Jorge, don't crack jokes.

FAT JORGE:
I'm being serious. What happened?

FLACA:
I'm sorry you were picked up.

FAT JORGE:
I'm sorry YOU were picked up.

FLACA:
Sometimes it's the price one pays. But one doesn't regret it.

They stare out the window again.

FAT JORGE:
Flaca.

FLACA:
Yes.

FAT JORGE:
They were telling the truth, weren't they?

FLACA:
Who?

FAT JORGE:
The secret police. When they were torturing me. They were telling the truth.

FLACA:
About what?

FAT JORGE:
About you.

FLACA:

That all depends.

FAT JORGE:

On what?

FLACA:

On how they worded it.

FAT JORGE:

"Your wife is a Marxist terrorist who's on her knees right now sucking her leader's cock."

FLACA:

Marxist.

FAT JORGE:

What does that mean?

FLACA:

You know how you always criticize the revolutionary movement?

FAT JORGE:

Well, yes, I used to—

FLACA:

That we're extremists—

FAT JORGE:

We?

FLACA:

That violence is never the solution, that we should all just sit down and talk things out—

FAT JORGE:

Yes—

FLACA:

I don't believe that. It would be so nice to believe that. So safe. But so blind. I couldn't turn a blind eye anymore.

FAT JORGE:

You believe in violence?

FLACA:

I believe in armed struggle.

FAT JORGE:

I see.

FLACA:

I no longer believe you can talk to the enemy. I believe you must fight him.

FAT JORGE:

Uh-huh.

FLACA:

Especially now.

FAT JORGE:

Because of what they did to you.

FLACA:

No. Because of what they're doing to our country. Because of what they're doing in Vietnam. Because of what they did in Guatemala.

FAT JORGE:

They said you were sucking your leader's cock and that you were responsible for a car bomb that killed a businessman from the American Embassy.

FLACA:

Businessman? That gringo was with the CIA and he came to train torturers. Anyway, that's not true. None of it is true. I was not involved in that. But I would die for what I believe in. And I would kill for it too.

FAT JORGE:

Right—

Scene Four

They are interrupted by the SOCIAL WORKER who enters with CRISTINA and ISABEL.

PAT:
Ici we are. *(seeing FAT JORGE and FLACA)* Oh! You two are still up! Excellent. Ici our new refugees! Do you know them? Amigos?

CRISTINA:
Where are we?

FAT JORGE:
In Canada.

FLACA:
Vancouver.

JOSELITO and MANUELITA descend the stairs.

MANUELITA:
What's your name?

The SOCIAL WORKER starts to ring the bell on the reception desk.

CRISTINA:
Cristina. I thought they were sending me to Toronto. *(to ISABEL)* Did you think you were going to Toronto?

ISABEL shrugs her shoulders.

CRISTINA:
Her name's Isabel.

The RECEPTIONIST enters.

PAT:
These are our next batch.

RECEPTIONIST:
(*handing the SOCIAL WORKER two separate keys, then referring to CRISTINA*) Love the poncho. Hand-woven alpaca.

He leaves.

PAT:
(*to FAT JORGE and FLACA*) Moi feliz tu are here. Tu make it mucho easier for the new arrivals to see some compatriots ici—

FAT JORGE:
(*nodding*) Jes jes.

CRISTINA:
What did she say?

FAT JORGE:
I have no clue. Just say jes jes to anything she says. It's called minding your manners. (*to CRISTINA*) Are you from Santiago?

CRISTINA:
No. I'm from the south. Mapuche. She's from Iquique. We just met on the plane.

FAT JORGE:
(*to ISABEL*) You don't talk, comrade?

ISABEL shakes her head no.

FLACA:
I see.

FAT JORGE:
Well, comrade, silence is underrated. You keep your words to yourself all you want. We'll call you Calladita: Little Silent One.

PAT:
Well, ici are the keys to your rooms. Your new casa. For el momento.

FAT JORGE:
Kids, let's help your aunties to their rooms! Just 'cause we're here doesn't mean you have to lose respect for your elders! Come on, let's go!

MANUELITA:
Aunt Calladita, can I hold your hand?

ISABEL nods. FAT JORGE and the kids take the women up to their rooms.

PAT:
Well! Moi so feliz this worked out!

FLACA:
Jes jes.

PAT:
Je ne sais pas if this means anything to you, my family and moi arrived from Hungary, in 1956. We're Jews—uh, not Cristianos (*crossing herself*)—

FLACA:
Ahhh! Cristiana!

SOCIAL WORKER:
No. No. NOT Cristianos. Jews. Anyway. And it meant a lot to have fellow Jews waiting for us when we landed—

FLACA hugs the SOCIAL WORKER.

Scene Five

FAT JORGE and the kids return from showing the two women to their rooms. The two kids go to the family's room. FLACA and FAT JORGE stay in the lobby.

FAT JORGE:
It was a week ago today that you would have been executed.

FLACA:
Me and the nine others.

FAT JORGE:
Would they have given us your body?

FLACA:
Oh, I'm sure they would have buried us all in the desert—

FAT JORGE:
And I would have spent the rest of my life looking for you.

FLACA:
I wouldn't have wanted that.

Pause.

FLACA:
I need you to know that I'm not sorry for any of it. Except for one thing: I'm sorry you were picked up.

FAT JORGE:
I've gotta ask you something.

FLACA:
Okay.

FAT JORGE:
When did you join the resistance?

FLACA:
Two years ago.

FAT JORGE:
Two years ago?!

FLACA:
At the university. You remember the day. My students had asked me to address the school on International Students' Day.

FAT JORGE:
I remember that day.

FLACA:
We all marched downtown and there were thousands of students and teachers from all over the city and Allende and Victor Jara and the leader of the Chilean Students' Federation were all there on the balcony of La Moneda Palace. Remember that we jumped so much and sang so loud we couldn't move the next day?

FAT JORGE:
You pulled a muscle and I lost my voice.

FLACA:
My students approached me after my speech and told me I had what it takes to be a revolutionary. After the celebration downtown, I knew I was ready. I had been asked to enter a room and I could never leave again. There was something bigger than me, than you, than us, than our country on that day. I understood why people give their lives. It had been easy to support Allende as long as there was no risk to take. Those days were gone and I knew we'd have to fight tooth and nail for what we'd achieved so far. It was an honour to be asked and when you are asked to give your life for a better world, you don't say no. You say yes. So I said yes. No matter what. Yes. But I couldn't tell you because I took an oath.

   The oath says that I will give my life to the cause. It says that I will not tell a soul. Not even my family. The oath talks about how if you are caught, you will not speak under torture. You will not give anyone away. Especially in the first twenty-four hours, when the torture is the worst. You will hang on to any information you have: a meeting point, an address, a licence plate number. You will not speak. And if they break you, only let them do so after enough time has passed to give your comrades the opportunity to run and hide. If you break and give people away easily, you agree to be executed by the leadership. Because you are a (coward.) A (traitor.)

politicizing   damage

FAT JORGE:
What about the kids? What about me?

FLACA:
Fat Jorge.

FAT JORGE:
Yes.

FLACA:
I'm not the same.

FAT JORGE:
But you still love me.

FLACA:
Fat Jorge.

FAT JORGE:
(*reaching for her*) What?—

FLACA:
(*catching him before he pulls her close to him*) They cut off my nipples.

Scene Six

Two days later. Morning. MANUELITA and JOSELITO watch My Favorite Martian *on TV. They sit very close to the TV, mouths agape.*

The RECEPTIONIST nods off at his desk.

On TV, Barbara, a hip Los Angeles secretary, enters her apartment to find Marty, a green man with antennae, sitting cross-legged on her loveseat.

BARBARA:
AAAAHHHH!

BARBARA faints.

MARTY:
Greetings, Earthling. I am Marty from Mars. I have travelled in my spaceship to come and study you specimens—

FAT JORGE enters. He is drenched.

FAT JORGE:
I just went into every restaurant up and down this street and said, "Me job"—

MANUELITA:
Shhh.

MARTY:
Very interesting. So you Earthlings arrive at your dwelling and immediately fall into a trance, much like we used to do ten thousand years ago—

FAT JORGE:
What the hell's up with the Martian?

43

JOSELITO:
He came into the lady's house and she fainted when she saw him.

FAT JORGE:
I can't believe these gringo shows. Anything to keep the people numb.

MANUELITA:
Huh?

FAT JORGE:
The comrades in jail explained it to me—

He turns off the TV.

JOSELITO and MANUELITA:
No! Papá! Papi!

FAT JORGE:
They make these stupid shows to keep their people numb. Where are the women?

MANUELITA:
Crying in their rooms.

FAT JORGE:
Oh, for fuck's sake. Again? Damn it's warm in here. One minute you're freezing in this country, the next you're boiling.

JOSELITO:
Mom went to buy some food. She told us to watch as much TV as possible so we could learn English.

FAT JORGE:
Yeah, right. By osmosis?

MANUELITA:
No. Just by listening. Real close.

FAT JORGE:
Look here, kids, these shows are designed to keep people from thinking about their world. Well, let me tell you, I could give a shit about outer space. Until the problems in this world are solved, I will give a shit about outer space.

JOSELITO:
But the Martian comes to Earth.

FAT JORGE:
Oh, yeah, and what a coincidence; the Martian comes to Earth and he lands right in the United States. Why doesn't he land in Chihuido del Medio? Why? Because Chihuido del Medio is in the so-called Third World and, according to these gringos, the Martian would only land in the centre of the world, which, according to them, is, let me guess, New York?

JOSELITO:
Maybe the Martian will land here next time.

FAT JORGE:
Maybe.

JOSELITO:
I'd like to talk to a Martian.

FAT JORGE:
So would I. 'Cause if I saw a Martian, I would ask him what it would be like to live in an anarchist society. 'Cause you gotta understand, kids, that if a creature from another planet were to land here on Earth, it would automatically mean that he is superior. Not just technologically, but in every way. Remember what I was telling you kids about the society we live in? Remember what it's called?

MANUELITA:
Capitalism.

FAT JORGE:
That's right, Manuelita. Capitalism. We live in a capitalist, imperialist society. We have a long way to go before the whole world is socialist. Centuries, really. And that dialectical process will take a lot of fighting from the masses. And once the whole world reaches socialism—which is, what, Joselito?

JOSELITO:
A classless society.

FAT JORGE:

That's right. And then, once the whole world is socialist, we will move towards communism and then towards anarchism. We've already gone through feudalism and now we're in the final phases of capitalism. The whole thing will come down and we will have to rebuild a socialist society—

MANUELITA:

What's anar-kism?

JOSELITO:

(*whispering*) Shut up.

FAT JORGE:

Anarchism is something you and I cannot even imagine, Manuelita. It's a state in which not only are everybody's basic needs met, but also, because everyone's nutritional needs are met, and everybody's in perfect health, and everybody has a good place to live, the human brain will naturally develop to its full capacity—'cause I already told you guys that we only use about two percent of our brain right now—and the human race will be able to live in peace and harmony. But that will only come through centuries of struggle, of liberating ourselves from oppression—

JOSELITO:

DAD! What does this have to do with the Martian?!

FAT JORGE:

Oh, right. The Martian. I would like to talk to the Martian too. Because the Martian is light years ahead of us, which automatically leads me to believe he lives in an anarchist society, and I would like to ask him about it. You know, converse. Converse with a man of the future. You children are very lucky that you have me to explain all of this to you. That your conscience can be born at such a tender age. That your conscience doesn't have to be born in jail.

FAT JORGE turns towards the Coke machine.

MANUELITA:

What's consc—(*JOSELITO covers her mouth with his hands. FAT JORGE doesn't hear her.*)

ISABEL and CRISTINA descend the stairs.

FAT JORGE:
> *(to the women)* Comrades. Man, I'm thirsty. *(arriving at the Coke machine)* How does this Coke machine work?

MANUELITA:
> *(muffled, through JOSELITO's hand)* I dunno.

> *FAT JORGE presses all the buttons on the machine. Finally, the Coke machine talks in a robot-like voice.*

COKE MACHINE:
> Feed me a coin, and I will give you a Coke.

FAT JORGE:
> How 'bout that? The thing talks. It's asking me what I want. You gotta admit these gringos have a sense of humour. *(to COKE MACHINE)* Coca-Cola! Coca-Cola! I want a Co-ca-Co-la! *(FAT JORGE waits. Nothing happens. He slaps the machine.)* Stupid thing doesn't even work.

> *FLACA enters with grocery bags. She is drenched.*

FAT JORGE:
> *(to CRISTINA and CALLADITA)* Comrades! You're going to take the kids on a stroll of Stanley's Park, aren't you?

CRISTINA:
> We are—?

JOSELITO and MANUELITA:
> Yayyyy!

FAT JORGE:
> *(shooing them out of the hotel)* Have a good one. Oh! And take your time!

Scene Seven

They leave. FLACA and FAT JORGE are alone.

FAT JORGE:
Let's go upstairs, my Mona Lisa—

FLACA:
I don't want to.

FAT JORGE:
Why?

FLACA:
I want us to talk.

FAT JORGE:
We'll talk too—

FLACA:
Are you going to tell me what you scream and puke about?

FAT JORGE:
I'm trying to tell you that I want to make love to you—

FLACA:
I don't want to.

FAT JORGE:
Flaca—

FLACA:
I don't want to! I have no nipples and my cunt hurts like hell.

FAT JORGE:
And we're never gonna touch each other again because of it?

FLACA:
I want us to talk.

FAT JORGE:
Flaquita, I want to see you.

FLACA:
I'm not ready to be seen. I wanna talk.

FAT JORGE:
What do you wanna talk about?

FLACA:
Everything. The reason we're here, the reason we left, the reason you scream, the reason I'm mutilated.

They stare at each other.

FLACA:
I want to know about the nightmare.

FAT JORGE shakes his head no.

FLACA:
Then talk to me about what it was like for you in jail.

FAT JORGE:
I can't.

FLACA:
After two years of not telling you about the resistance, of being in the concentration camp for five months, thinking I would never see you or the kids again, I believe that the place to start is by talking. Otherwise it means they've destroyed us.

FAT JORGE:
They may have destroyed me, Flaca, but let me tell you one thing. I learned more about the world in those few weeks than in my entire life. And I may have lost everything, but I gained something that I never knew I had: my conscience. I died in jail, Flaquita. I fucking died. But my conscience was born. Shit. Now you're gonna make me start crying.

FLACA:
Is that so bad?

FAT JORGE:
Yes, Flaca, yes. It would be bad.

[handwritten left margin: that → conscience perpetuates his episodes]

[handwritten bottom: Much of that conscience is grounded in guilt; relive his traumatic experiences with 50 an added pang of guilt]

FLACA:
Why?

FAT JORGE:
Do revolutionaries cry?

FLACA:
Yes. And they ask a lot of questions. Come on. Ask me a question. I need to know that you can stand this. You want to be a revolutionary? Well, the revolution starts right here. Right now.

Pause.

FAT JORGE:
Don't tell me about the torture.

FLACA:
Start by asking me something you can stand. But start. Somewhere. Now.

Pause.

FAT JORGE:
Um. Dawson Island. Okay. You were in Dawson Island. With who? Who else was there?

FLACA:
With the crème de la crème. All the union leaders, the party leaders, the students, the actors, the miners, the priests. I was with them. God I miss them.

FAT JORGE:
Don't cry.

FLACA:
I'm not crying. I'm talking. I don't know how you dealt with it, Fat Jorge, because you weren't involved. But I was. I sat on the plane, handcuffed to that seat, my heart pounding. I hadn't seen you and the kids for so long. Months. Centuries. Lifetimes upon lifetimes. Then you came down the aisle and when I saw you I just ...

FAT JORGE:
What?

FLACA:

You were like a mirror. You've changed so much. When I saw your eyes look at me, I saw the reflection of how much I've changed.

FAT JORGE:

My Mona Lisa.

Pause.

FLACA:

What do you scream and puke about?

FAT JORGE:

The time spent there.

FLACA:

What? Talk to me.

FAT JORGE:

I can't.

FLACA:

Okay.

CALLADITA, CRISTINA, MANUELITA, and JOSELITO enter. They are drenched.

CRISTINA:

Every time I leave this place I don't see a soul.

JOSELITO:

They're all in their cars!

MANUELITA:

Were you crying, Mom?

FLACA:

No. But, hey! Why don't we all go to our room? I'll make us some milk with tea and I'll teach you some of the card games I learned in Dawson Island.

JOSELITO:

Yayyy!

They all start going up the stairs.

FLACA:
We'll start with Mao-Mao. The key to the game is that every time you're finished your move you say: Mao-Mao.

CRISTINA:
As opposed to Ho Chi Minh-Ho Chi Minh?

FLACA:
That's another game. The leader of the copper miners' unions taught it to me. We called him Titicaco 'cause he was full-blooded Aymara Indian; it was like looking into the very heart of the highlands when you looked in his eyes. He taught me so many great games, I don't want to forget them. We'll start with Mao-Mao, move on to Run, Che, Run and continue with Go Tupac Amaru.

Scene Eight

PAT enters with MANUEL. He is wearing a poncho. His head is shaved. He looks like a skeleton. PAT rings the bell on the desk. The RECEPTIONIST appears.

PAT:
(*to the RECEPTIONIST*) This one's called Manuel Iturra.

RECEPTIONIST:
You didn't tell me about this one.

PAT:
He's come directly from a concentration camp in the Atacama desert—

RECEPTIONIST:
Please. No details.

PAT:
Set him up while I get a doctor.

RECEPTIONIST:
Okay.

The RECEPTIONIST takes MANUEL to his room and goes back to his counter. He breaks down and cries. Everyone else plays cards in FLACA and FAT JORGE's room. CALLADITA comes down the stairs. She picks up the pay phone and listens to the dial tone. As the sound of the dial tone fills the theatre, PAT arrives with the DOCTOR. The DOCTOR goes to MANUEL's room; the RECEPTIONIST and PAT stay behind. When the DOCTOR arrives, MANUEL takes his clothes off. The DOCTOR performs a physical on him.

MANUEL:

Cigarette burns. Blow torches. Electricity. Many blows to the head. Heart failure. Brought back to life. Fingernails pulled out. Raped by men. Raped by dogs. Electricity. To the gums. To the eyes. To the tongue. To the anus. To the testicles. Starvation. Dehydration. Hypothermia. Solitary confinement. Many, many, many blows to the head. And I'm alive.

The DOCTOR places a stethoscope to MANUEL's heart. The sound of a beating heart fills the theatre. The lone male CUECA DANCER emerges, doing the zapateo in the background.

MANUEL:

I'm alive.

Celebration of survival →avoiding talk of the damaged person

The DOCTOR leaves. MANUEL continues to stand, naked.

The CUECA DANCER continues to dance.

Scene Nine

*Two days later. CALLADITA, FLACA, FAT JORGE,
CRISTINA, JOSELITO, MANUELITA, and MANUEL
descend the stairs. MANUEL is aided by the CUECA
DANCER, who is invisible to everyone else. The
RECEPTIONIST is at his desk.*

FLACA:
(*to MANUEL*) Need any help?

MANUEL shakes his head no.

MANUELITA:
I bet there's finally a letter from Grandma.

JOSELITO:
I don't see why we have to check the mail every day. It'll take a
month for a letter to get here.

FLACA:
Because it's a ritual. And those are important.

MANUELITA:
Uncle Manuel, can I hold your hand?

MANUEL nods.

BILL O'NEILL enters. He is drenched.

JOSELITO:
Hey! (*pointing at BILL*) Look at that hippie!

FLACA:
(*to JOSELITO*) Don't point.

BILL:
How beauty to look you! Me can't believe this! Me feel like I'm in Chile once more!

MANUELITA:
You're not. You're in Canada.

FAT JORGE:
I can't believe it! I can't believe it! You're the first gringo we meet here who speaks Spanish and there's so many things we need to talk about, comrade.

BILL:
(*to the Chileans*) Me Bill. Just got back of Santiago. Hear me, me spend four weeks on the National Stadium and then four weeks on Chile Stadium—

CRISTINA:
Shit.

BILL:
Shit is correct. Me thumb, uh, climb?

CRISTINA:
Hitchhike!

BILL:
Yes. Yes. Hitchhike. South America. Hitchhike Chile as coup take place. Arrested for long hair and beard. Fifty-six days in camps of concentrations and me learn that life is intense, precious, like jewel.

I find out you chilis here and I come down to look at you immediately. Me want to let you understand that many, many gringos in solidarity with you chilis and we provide couches— no, um, support—anything you desire. Not just gringos. The Palestinians wants express their fraternal hellos—

MANUEL:
Did you see Galindo Rodríguez in Chile Stadium?

BILL:
Uh—

MANUEL:

What about Carmen Rojas?

BILL:

Okay, me look at too many people—

MANUEL:

You must have seen Emilio Moreno and his wife Matilde—

BILL:

That names sound familiars, but me has very many names on my head, you understand—

MANUEL:

I just want to know if they're still alive, or what happened to them—

FLACA:

Calm down, Manuel. The poor man has just arrived and we haven't even offered him a seat.

CRISTINA puts her hand on MANUEL's back and rubs it.

BILL:

No, no. Me understand. Me assemble list with help of Interfaith Church, they wants get people out of Chile soon possible, you have names to sprinkle on list?—

FLACA:

Please, sit down. Make yourself at home.

BILL:

Hear me, me acquire name of government workperson on your case. Me investigate your situation. Me inform you.

FAT JORGE:

All I know is that this is a hotel we're staying in and I know that hotels are expensive. I've never stayed in a hotel. Ever in my life. And now here we are for five nights already and we don't have a penny to pay for it. So we've been looking for jobs but to no avail—

BILL:

Oh, God me. You NO pay for hotel—

JOSELITO:
Told ya!

BILL:

Don't be nervous. Me speak on the worker. Me speak on the receptionist and inform you. (*opening his backpack, pulling out a bottle of wine*) But right now, time celebrate our arrival on Canada. Look me!

ALL THE ADULT CHILEANS:
Wine!

BILL:

Yes. (*to the RECEPTIONIST*) Come join us. No Chilean however. We boycott Chilean wine, correct?

FAT JORGE:
Of course, comrade.

BILL:
Italian.

The RECEPTIONIST brings glasses. BILL pours the wine for everybody.

BILL:
I'll get the kids some pop.

BILL buys two Cokes from the vending machine.

FAT JORGE:

So that's how the stupid thing works! Shoulda known. You have to pay for everything in this country. Capitalism is—

FLACA:

Fat Jorge, don't start with one of your speeches. (*to BILL*) You have to forgive him. You see, his conscience was born in prison, and now he has to keep trying it out all the time.

BILL:
Me. I the same.

FLACA and BILL share a look.

BILL:
You are Camila Urrutia?

FLACA:

Yes, I am.

BILL:

Oh, God me. You're ... (*choosing his words carefully, aware that her children are in the room*) You're ... well, you be example. There be many stories about you in the prisoners. You know, about the pain you endure and in spite you keep all information inside, give nobody away ... You resistance symbol ... Excuse me: you not be executed one week ago?

FLACA:

I was headed for the firing squad with the nine others and then all of a sudden the blindfold gets taken off and I'm loaded into a helicopter, then into a military vehicle, and then a Canadian embassy car, driven for twenty-four hours straight to Santiago airport, taken to a plane and handcuffed.

FAT JORGE:

We were waiting to enter the plane, where she was supposed to be waiting for us, but I never thought it was true.

FLACA:

And then there they all were. Walking down the aisle. My kids were so big and my husband was almost skinny!

MANUELITA:

He's always throwing up.

JOSELITO:

Shhhh.

BILL:

Oh, comrades. My heart is big with you. (*holding up his drink*) Me want welcome you chilis to Canada, my country. Me toast you for survive, for come here, for enrich my country with your wisdom. Me want you stay on many years, but me hopes that Pinochet fall and you return your homeland much sooner than later!

FAT JORGE:

A toast! To us, to you, to the old gringo, to the refugee hotel!

They all drink.

CRISTINA:
(*to MANUEL, intimately*) And to you, the martyr of Chacabuco.

ALL THE CHILEANS and BILL:
Salud!

Scene Ten

*Later that night. Everyone is asleep in their rooms. FAT
JORGE, drunk, has fallen asleep on the couch. His nightmare
continues. The lights change. He gets up and takes on a position
as if he's hanging by his wrists from the ceiling. FLACA, in the
family's room, takes on the position of a woman hanging, as if
crucified, from a wall. MANUEL, in his room, takes on the
"man" character, also hanging. The remainder of the cast
moans and weeps.*

MAN:
Tortured you badly.

FAT JORGE:
Yeah.

MAN:
Got you on the street?

FAT JORGE:
No. At the bank.

MAN:
Bank of America?

FAT JORGE:
Bank of Chile.

MAN:
So. We're robbing national banks now too.

FAT JORGE:
Robbing?

MAN:
Was your whole cell caught?

FAT JORGE:
Uh—

MAN:
Or just you?

FAT JORGE:
I was working at the bank and—I'm an accountant—and they raided the place. I think they wanted the guy who works at the desk next to mine. He's been missing for days—

MAN:
You weren't robbing the bank?

FAT JORGE:
No! I'm not a common criminal—

MAN:
I mean for the cause.

FAT JORGE:
The cause?

MAN:
Robbing the bank as a revolutionary, anti-imperialist act—

FAT JORGE:
I don't know what you're talking about.

MAN:
They wanted your colleague.

FAT JORGE screams, runs to the window, opens it and pukes. FLACA runs down the stairs.

FLACA:
(*rubbing his back*) It's okay, my little big bear, everything's going to be okay.

Scene Eleven

Everyone in the hotel, having heard the scream, is coming down the stairs. The RECEPTIONIST comes to the desk. BILL O'Neill enters with JUAN. They are both drenched.

BILL:
Comrades!

FLACA:
Oh, hello, Bill.

JOSELITO:
Bill O'Neill!

MANUELITA:
(*to JUAN*) What's your name?

JUAN:
Juan. Reyes—

MANUELITA:
I'm Manuelita.

CRISTINA:
Are you staying here too?

JUAN:
I don't know, I just ran away from the jail in Valparaíso and—

FAT JORGE:
You ran away from the jail in Valparaíso?!

JUAN:
Yeah—

FLACA:
Please, make yourself at home—

JUAN:

Thank you. It was during a transfer, actually. I slipped out of the van and ran for my life. Next thing I know, I'm sharing my meals with rats at the bottom of a freighter—

JOSELITO:

Like a ship?

JUAN:

Huge ship and—

BILL:

Me come rapid to port because my mother tell me she saw news say that chili found hiding in Swedish ship here on harbour and they want deport him back on Chile. So my mother give me keys for her station wagon and I arrive there soon possible so help him—

FAT JORGE:

Keys for what?

BILL:

Station wa—car.

JUAN:

Yeah, I'm standing there with all these reporters blinding me with their flashes and these gringo cops built like tractors and two heads taller than me and this hippie arrives in this car like that show about that family with the six kids—

JOSELITO:

Wow!

FAT JORGE:

(*to JUAN*) You're my hero. You are my hero, comrade. Ha! He runs away from the jail during a transfer and ends up with the Swedes! Ha!

CRISTINA runs upstairs to her room to get the bottle of pisco.

JUAN:

(*to BILL*) Am I going to be deported?

BILL:

No absolutely.

FLACA:
No! That would be absolutely criminal!

BILL:
Me make sure you not fucking deportation. I sit on the Immigration Ministry with me friends.

FLACA:
(to JUAN) Sit down.

CRISTINA:
What did you do in Valparaíso, comrade?

JUAN:
I was with the railway. Railworkers' Union. Beautiful job. To see that railway stretch out before you. And behind you. So sensual. So complete. And it requires a great deal of knowledge, too. You've gotta know about algebra, about trigonometry. You've gotta know about cables. My father was in the union. I started work on the railway when I was a kid. Right after the country got electrified. We rail workers have a great deal of power in the country. We can shut everything down. Or start everything up. I've gotta get a job. Fast. I've gotta send money to my girlfriend. Her and I met in the choir. (sings) La Chueca has the voice of an angel. I call her La Chueca 'cause her legs go like this. I've gotta bring her here. (going towards pay phone) Oh, good. Here's a phone. I've gotta call her and tell her to pack her bags—

FLACA:
You've gotta wind down, Juan. You're still shaking. You just got here. Relax.

FAT JORGE:
We'll go on a job search tomorrow—

JUAN:
Right after I call her—

FAT JORGE:
(to JUAN, referring to job search) —You, me, and Manuel.

BILL:
No, you no need go on job search—

JUAN:

(*still referring to phone call*) Is it the same day in Chile tomorrow?

CRISTINA:

(*handing out the drinks to everyone*) The ultimate: pisco made by the Artesanos of Cochiguáz.

JUAN:

Holy Mary, Mother of God.

FAT JORGE:

(*to CRISTINA*) And you've been keeping this from us for five days? (*holding up glass*) A toast to our comrade the railworker, the brave and valiant revolutionary who risked his life—

JUAN:

(*holding up glass*) Chi Chi Chi le le le.

EVERYONE:

VI-VA CHI-LE!

Scene Twelve

Later that same night. FAT JORGE, FLACA, JOSELITO,
MANUELITA, CALLADITA, JUAN, BILL, and CRISTINA
are still in the lobby of the hotel. The adults are drinking pisco.
MANUEL is in his room. The RECEPTIONIST is not at his
desk.

FLACA:
We won't be in this hotel for long—

FAT JORGE:
We'll all find jobs, we'll pay the bill—

BILL:
No. You no pay no bill here—

FAT JORGE:
And we'll all find a house together—

FLACA:
And we'll go back as soon as Pinochet falls.

CALLADITA sadly shakes her head no.

FLACA:
What's that, comrade?

CALLADITA shakes her head no.

CRISTINA:
I don't see it getting any better in the next few months—

JUAN:
You'll have to light a candle to Saint Teresa of the Andes if you
want old Pinocchio to fall anytime soon—

FLACA:

But people are fighting to topple—

CRISTINA:

Comrade, you've been in Dawson Island, practically in Antarctica, since the coup, surrounded by heroes, so you have a romantic notion of what's going on: Chileans are cowering in their houses. I've come to the conclusion that our country is a country of cowards—

FAT JORGE:

Comrade! How dare you!

CRISTINA:

It's true, Fat Jorge. We live in a country of cowards and until we find our balls, nothing will change! You hear me? Nothing!

FAT JORGE:

Don't spit on the memory of the martyrs, comrade; I won't allow it!

CRISTINA:

I'm not talking about the martyrs! I'm talking about the rest of the country that sits around and turns the other way when their neighbours are being taken away in broad daylight!

FAT JORGE:

Nobody's turning away! Who's turning away?

CRISTINA:

The whole goddamned country is turning away! Comrade Allende starts the day by giving his life for the country, and most people, what do they do? Nothing!

FLACA:

That's 'cause they don't have arms to fight with, sister!

JUAN:

It's true: all I had was a slingshot my cockeyed cousin gave me, and that was it—

CRISTINA:

I don't care!

JUAN:
La Chueca stole her great-grandfather's pistol from the War of the Pacific, but it didn't work—

CRISTINA:
I don't care!

FLACA:
Terror paralyzes, Cristina. Terror eats away like cancer—

JUAN:
There's nothing worse than fear. Fear is the mind-killer.

CRISTINA:
I don't care! If you're sitting in your house and you see your neighbours being taken away, beaten, burnt, the house ransacked, do you sit there and shake like a goddamn leaf? When the day before you shared a cup of tea with that very neighbour? Do you?

MANUELITA:
My grandma attacked the military with her broom!

FLACA:
And almost got herself killed! You cannot fight their machinery with brooms or rocks or Molotov cocktails!

CRISTINA:
We did! The Mapuches did! And we had nothing when the Spaniards arrived! We fought them, with whatever we had, and they did not beat us!

FLACA:
These are different times, comrade; you know the gringos are involved—

CRISTINA:
Of course I know the gringos are involved!

FLACA:
What you're saying is that we should declare war on the military, and that's what I'm saying too, comrade, but to fight a war you need arms, you need people, you need to get organized—

CRISTINA:

I'm saying that if your neighbours are being taken away in front of your face you grab whatever you can, whatever's at hand—an ax, a knife, a·piece of furniture, a broom—and if every last person in the neighbourhood does it and storms the soldiers every single time they do it, what's happening in Chile right now wouldn't be happening!

FAT JORGE:

But then you're assuming that everyone in the neighbourhood is unified as one, and, as we now see, there were traitors amongst us all along, all along—

JUAN:

True. True. Turns out La Chueca's uncle twice-removed was an informer.

CRISTINA:

Who can you trust? Who?

BILL:

Me not know.

CRISTINA:

How could they just sit and watch? How?

JOSELITO:

Who?

CRISTINA:

They just sat and watched my parents being taken away. Nobody helped; they just sat and watched like they were watching TV—

JOSELITO:

(confused) TV?

CRISTINA:

My parents. They took them away and the neighbours, all of them, the very ones that saw me being born just sat and watched. I was at the craft market, trying to sell some pottery, that's all—

CALLADITA is slowly rocking.

MANUELITA:
What's she doing, Mommy?

FLACA:
Nothing. She's just comforting herself.

FAT JORGE is drinking. A lot.

FAT JORGE:
I refuse to believe that Chile's done for. I refuse, I don't care if I have to go sneak back in tomorrow, I don't care about the fucking blacklist—

CALLADITA keeps rocking.

FLACA:
(getting up) Fat Jorge, you're drunk.

FAT JORGE:
I see it clearly now! Thank you, comrade Cristina, for the clarity! I see it so well! Here we are, in a hotel, a HOTEL—that's just too fucking ironic—in a goddamn hotel, in the heart of the monster, as refugees, REFUGEES, do you hear me? Since when do refugees stay in hotels and watch TV and learn English? I see it now! This is all a set-up! That's what it is! Exiles, my ass. If we had balls, we'd be there, we'd be living in the underground, helping out. I'm leaving. Come on! Get up! All of you! You too, comrade Bill! We're leaving this place right now!

FLACA:
We are doing no such thing! Fat Jorge, for the last time, sit down and shut up or I'll have to slap you! You're scaring the kids and the old gringo's gonna kick us out. In fact, kids, I want you to go upstairs to bed—

FAT JORGE:
No! You two kids stay right here and listen to all this! Keep your eyes open. Keep your ears open. Look. Listen. Very carefully. This is life. And you've gotta be present for it. You've gotta be.

CRISTINA:
This is life? This hotel?

FLACA:
We'll be out of here in no time. In no time. You'll see. Come on. We're all going to bed. Fat Jorge, you first. Let's go.

FAT JORGE:
I can't stay here, Flaquita. I can't. Everything smells the same here. They spray everything. (to CRISTINA) And you! You call our people cowards? What about you? If you're so goddamn brave, then why did you leave? Why?

CRISTINA:
They killed my parents.

FAT JORGE:
So you leave? Just like that?

CRISTINA:
No! Not just like that!

FLACA:
Fat Jorge, don't.

FAT JORGE:
Why didn't you stay and join the underground?

CRISTINA:
You white-ass fuck! You live your cushy life in downtown Santiago and now all of a sudden 'cause you found out there's a fence that divides the rich from the poor, now all of a sudden 'cause you decided to jump to the side of the fence that the rest of us have always been on, now all of a sudden you can look me in the eye with no shame whatsoever and ask me why I love life so much that I decided to live it?! Fuck you.

FAT JORGE:
Answer the question.

FLACA:
Leave her alone, Fat Jorge. Can't you see she's a kid?

CRISTINA:
(to FAT JORGE) 'Cause I'm scared. Okay? You satisfied now? 'Cause I'm so scared that I haven't slept or eaten for months and I was afraid of myself. Afraid of what I might do. I was

afraid of turning into a traitor. From sheer fear. So when I saw the opportunity to run, I ran, okay? Satisfied? Now, you may know a little bit about fear, comrade. But I know a lot about it. I am a Mapuche. We've lived in fear for 450 years. And I've seen what fear can do. It can turn you into a traitor or into a hero.

MANUELITA:
What's a traitor?

FLACA:
It's when you give away your friends to the enemy because your spirit breaks.

MANUELITA:
Oh.

FAT JORGE:
(to CRISTINA) You did the right thing, comrade.

CRISTINA:
Do you think my spirit is broken?

CALLADITA shakes her head no.

CRISTINA:
Maybe I should just kill myself.

FLACA:
Don't talk like that, comrade. If you kill yourself it will mean you have surrendered to the enemy.

CRISTINA:
But fleeing means I've surrendered to the enemy.

FLACA:
You chose life over death.

CALLADITA nods.

FAT JORGE:
She's not a traitor. But I am, Flaquita. I am. I'm here when I could be there. Oh my God. (running helplessly around the room) I'm stuck here. I'm stuck here. I'm stuck here ...

FAT JORGE keeps running around the room. BILL and JUAN physically restrain him. FAT JORGE holds on to his gut so he won't puke.

FLACA:
(*leading the kids up the stairs*) Come on, kids, let's go. Quickly!

BILL and JUAN lead FAT JORGE up the stairs.

FLACA:
Cristina, Calladita, let's go. No more talking. Let's go.

BILL, JUAN, FAT JORGE, FLACA, JOSELITO, and MANUELITA end up in the family's room. CRISTINA goes to her room and paces.

MANUEL:
(*in his room, looking out the window*)Is it possible to have lived too long at the age of seventeen? Santiago in the spring, that first kiss on that bench in the Quinta Normal, the school trip to Antofagasta, my mother slaving away at the RCA Victor factory. I remember the day Allende won, the march with my school, down the Alameda, to La Moneda Palace, Comrade Allende, the people united will never be defeated! ¡El pueblo unido jamás será vencido! And now I'm here. And I can't breathe. Or think. Or see. And enough is enough. Enough is enough. ¡Ya basta ya! Basta. My mother used to say, nothing belongs to us, Manuel. Absolutely nothing. Not even our bodies. We come from the dirt and when we die we go back to the dirt.

MANUEL jumps. He flies by the family's window, in slow motion, free-falling. They all stare, stupefied, unable to move, in a state of shock. CALLADITA and JUAN also see him fly by.

FAT JORGE:
That was Manuel! That crazy bastard just killed himself!

FAT JORGE and BILL run out of the room. The kids start to follow. FLACA holds them back. JUAN and CALLADITA run after FAT JORGE and BILL.

FLACA:
No! We're staying here!

FLACA embraces the children. They all stand in silence.
Holding on to each other.

JOSELITO:
Why did he do that mommy?

FLACA:
Sometimes sadness overtakes you, like a flood.

MANUELITA:
Is he dead?

FLACA:
I don't know, Manuelita. I don't know.

The three of them continue to embrace. Lights go down on
their room, and come up on CRISTINA's, next door. She is
pacing in her kitchenette.

CRISTINA:
Is it possible to feel too much? I want to kill them all. If I could
only make a Molotov cocktail right now and kill all those
fucking sons of bitches. Where's my mommy? Where's my
daddy? Are you here with me? God help me. You fucking
asshole. If you existed, God, I wouldn't be here right now, north
of the Equator, without my mommy and daddy. I'm sorry. I'm
sorry I'm not there to take flowers to your graves. I'm sorry I'm
here in this place full of barf-coloured rugs. Dear God, I think
I'm going to die. Mommy. Daddy. Remember me? The squishy
little girl with the fuzzy braids and skinned knees? I need you
now. Is it possible to have lived too long at the age of eighteen?
I think it is.

CRISTINA turns the oven on full blast and sticks her head in.

Lights come up on FLACA, MANUELITA, and JOSELITO.
FAT JORGE returns.

FAT JORGE:
He's not dead. He's alive. He fell three storeys and the lucky
son of a bitch is alive.

FLACA:
What?

FAT JORGE:
He fell inside a huge rectangular garbage can full of pink cotton—

FLACA:
Have you lost your mind?

MANUELITA:
He's in heaven!

FAT JORGE:
No! He fell inside this huge square garbage can! And inside it is this pink cotton stuff, like cotton candy! He fell inside it! Didn't even break a nail!

FLACA:
Jesus Christ. He must feel like an idiot.

MANUELITA:
He's in heaven!

FAT JORGE:
No! He's in the street!

FLACA:
Let's go help him—

MANUELITA:
Mommy, what's that smell?

FLACA:
What smell?

JOSELITO:
Something's burning—

FAT JORGE:
He's right. Something's burning.

FLACA:
It's hair. It's burning hair.

CRISTINA still has her head stuck in the oven. Smoke is all around her. FAT JORGE, FLACA, MANUELITA, and JOSELITO run out into the hallway.

MANUELITA:
It's coming from here!

JOSELITO:
Yeah! It's from Auntie Cristina's room!

FAT JORGE walks right into the room. Everyone follows. They see CRISTINA with her head in the oven, surrounded by smoke.

FAT JORGE:
Holy shit.

They run to her and pull her out. Her hair is burnt. Her face is black.

FAT JORGE:
Woman! If you're gonna commit suicide like that, at least make sure it's a gas oven!

JOSELITO:
Yeah! This is electric!

MANUELITA:
Your hair's burnt.

JOSELITO:
And your face is all black!

FLACA:
Would everybody just shut up and take pity on the poor girl?

CRISTINA:
Shit. This is an electric oven?

FLACA:
Yeah.

CRISTINA:
How the hell was I supposed to know that?

FAT JORGE:
Don't worry, comrade. Manuel just tried to kill himself, too. You're not alone.

MANUEL enters, escorted by BILL, CALLADITA, and JUAN.

FAT JORGE:
Here's your comrade in the struggle!

CRISTINA:
You just tried to kill yourself too?

MANUEL:
Yeah.

CRISTINA:
At the precise moment when I was trying to kill myself?

MANUEL:
Yeah.

FAT JORGE:
Hey! We'll have to call you Condor Passes! Flying by our window like that like the King of the Andes. And you! Wanting to bake your head like that! We'll just have to call you Cakehead!

MANUEL starts to laugh. They all laugh.

FAT JORGE:
You lonely fuckers. You lonely fuckers.

They all stand in a circle and laugh. FAT JORGE breaks the circle. Everyone continues laughing. FAT JORGE is in his own world. The CUECA DANCER is there.

ACT TWO

Scene One

The next day. "Pollera colorada" plays, mixed in with a soundscape of wind. FLACA, FAT JORGE, and JOSELITO are frozen in a tableau in the lobby. ADULT MANUELITA dances with the CUECA DANCER, who introduces her to the tableau. She joins the tableau and we are in the past again.

FAT JORGE takes FLACA by the hands and starts dancing with her. The kids dance with each other. Music fades out.

FAT JORGE:
(*creating "pollera colorada" music with his voice*) Come on, Flaquita, move those hips! (*continues to create "pollera colorada" music with his voice*)

FLACA:
(*crying*) I can't, Fat Jorge, I can't—

JOSELITO:
(*dancing with MANUELITA*) Why's Mommy crying, Dad?

FAT JORGE:
(*still dancing with FLACA, who allows herself to be led*) She's sad today, Joselito. Just sad. Sadness overtakes everything sometimes, and you just gotta keep dancing till it passes, kids. Dancing till it passes. And it will pass.

MANUELITA:
(*dancing with JOSELITO*) I'm hungry.

FLACA:
(*crying uncontrollably*) I'll make breakfast. Fry you an egg and make you some tea with condensed milk, like your grandma

used to, back in Chile ... (*weeping, still dancing with FAT JORGE*) Remember? Remember Grandma with her wood stove and the smell of fresh bread and the vineyard giving grapes this fat—

MANUELITA:
Yeah, and the peach kuchen—

JOSELITO:
Mmm!

FAT JORGE:
(*running towards kids and dancing with them too*) Flaca! You're gonna make me and the kids cry too! Jesus! We held it together with the suicide attempts last night but all this talk of food and beverage will do us in! Come on! Everybody dance together!

The four of them dance. The kids giggle as FAT JORGE dances over-the-top cumbia and FLACA dances and laughs through her tears.

FAT JORGE:
(*still dancing*) If we'd only thought of bringing "The Greatest Cumbias of All Time."

MANUELITA:
I told you to bring all your records!

FAT JORGE:
And I should have listened to you, you precious princess you! I guess we'll just have to form our own cumbia band so we can dance dance dance!

MANUELITA:
Can I be in the cumbia band?

The CUECA DANCER appears with a record of Inti-Illimani. FAT JORGE takes it from him.

FAT JORGE:
(*showing off the record*) Why form a band when we've got this?

The whole family gasps.

Scene Two

JUAN, CONDOR PASSES, CALLADITA, and CAKEHEAD appear in the lobby. The RECEPTIONIST is vacuuming. FAT JORGE holds the Inti-Illimani record.

FAT JORGE:
Excuse me! Excuse me!

The RECEPTIONIST continues vacuuming.

FAT JORGE:
(*standing in front of the RECEPTIONIST, waving his arms around*) Excuse me!

RECEPTIONIST:
(*turning off vacuum cleaner*) What is it this time?

He sees the whole group standing there, smiling expectantly.

FAT JORGE:
(*showing record*) Uh, we were wondering if you have a record player for us to listen to this—

RECEPTIONIST:
I don't understand what you're saying!

FAT JORGE:
This is a beautiful record of gorgeous Andean music with outstanding revolutionary lyrics by one of Chile's top folk groups, which is now completely banned in our homeland, and it has miraculously fallen from the sky into my hands. This record is a symbol of resistance. The fact that this record is here, at the refugee hotel, just sitting here, shaking in my hands, is enough to move the masses of the world because we want to listen to a song by Víctor Jara, that holy martyr who was

brutally murdered by the regime for the simple yet indisputable fact that Víctor Jara was a poor man who wrote lyrics that spoke to the people, that were of the people, that gave dignity to the working man. And this record, this record means so much to us, the fact that it's here, and that so many are not. So I stand here, with this humble yet noble record in my hands, I stand here in this new country and I ask you if you will please lend us a record player—don't worry, we won't break it—so we can listen to "El Aparecido," tribute to Che Guevara, written by Víctor Jara, both of whom are now dead, dead in the hands of traitors, of fascists, of right-wing pigs who destroy life in the name of profit. Please, let us listen to "El Aparecido."

RECEPTIONIST:
I'll get you a record player right away.

The RECEPTIONIST leaves and returns immediately with a record player. He sets it up.

CONDOR PASSES:
(*to CAKEHEAD, proudly*) RCA Victor. I made the needles for those. At the factory in Santiago.

FAT JORGE pulls the record out of its cover and hands it to the RECEPTIONIST. The RECEPTIONIST puts it on. "El Aparecido" begins to play. Everyone listens in silence. MANUEL raises his left fist. The others follow, except for JOSELITO. The RECEPTIONIST listens intently.

FAT JORGE:
(*once song is over*) Thank you. That song is banned in Chile right now.

RECEPTIONIST:
That's remarkable music! Thank you for letting me listen to it! We'll keep the record player here now, by the lava lamp. You can listen to your records all you want. All you want. Remarkable music. Remarkable.

Scene Three

*Later that night. Everyone is asleep in their rooms. FAT
JORGE sings the Inti-Illimani song in the lobby, wine bottle in
hand. His nightmare continues. He takes on the same
position, of being hung by the wrists from the ceiling. FLACA
and MANUEL also take on the same shapes as before. The
cast help to create the soundscape by moaning, coughing,
praying, and weeping.*

WOMAN (*played by* FLACA):
   Where are we?

MAN:
   In the bowels of this country.

Scene Four

FAT JORGE wakes up screaming. He runs to the window in the lobby, opens it, and pukes. FLACA runs down the stairs.

FLACA:
Are you okay?

FAT JORGE:
Yeah, I'm alright.

Pause.

FLACA:
Maybe if you talk about it you won't dream about it anymore.

FAT JORGE:
I won't talk about it.

FLACA:
Where's this new man you say you've become?

FAT JORGE:
I won't talk about it. I can't take it.

FLACA:
Fat Jorge, you MUST take it.

FAT JORGE:
Jesus Christ, woman, can't you see I'm weak?! Look at me, woman, I'm weak! I'm not like you!

FLACA:
We're all different—

FAT JORGE:
No. I'm not talking about differences. I'm talking about fucking weakness.

FLACA:

I was more prepared for what happened than you—

FAT JORGE:

Woman, understand what I'm trying to tell you: if I had taken that oath I would have broken it. Fast.

FLACA:

I—

FAT JORGE:

I'm like a child, a broken bone—

FLACA:

And if you don't deal with what happened—

FAT JORGE:

Flaca, I'm a traitor.

FLACA:

Because we're in exile?

FAT JORGE:

No.

Pause.

FLACA:

You broke.

FAT JORGE nods.

FLACA:

You gave someone away.

FAT JORGE:

Time stood still. Or went on forever. I don't know. I couldn't tell.

FLACA:

Who did you give away?

FAT JORGE:

I told them about my colleague.

FLACA:

What did you tell them?

FAT JORGE:
He's the one they wanted. I told them details of his family. Of his hang-outs. Of his life.

FLACA:
You mean Cesar?

FAT JORGE nods.

FAT JORGE:
It must have worked. 'Cause they let me go after that.

FLACA:
They probably would have found him anyway—

FAT JORGE:
I don't know. All I know is that by that time I had to talk.

FLACA:
Everybody talked, Fat Jorge, everybody. No one was prepared for what happened.

FAT JORGE:
Except you. You were prepared.

FLACA:
No, I wasn't.

FAT JORGE:
You didn't talk.

FLACA:
I couldn't.

FAT JORGE:
But I could. And I did.

FLACA:
We're here now, Fat Jorge. Here.

FLACA goes to the bedroom. After a moment, FAT JORGE follows.

Scene Five

Much later that night. All the adults are asleep. MANUELITA and JOSELITO are in the lobby of the hotel. JOSELITO has the telephone receiver in one hand, Pat Kelemen's business card in the other. He has his suitcase.

JOSELITO:
I took that lady's card from Mom's purse. She'll help us.

MANUELITA:
You have to pay for that phone.

JOSELITO:
No, you don't.

MANUELITA:
Do so. You have to pay for everything here. It's called capitalism.

JOSELITO:
(mocking) "It's called capitalism—"

MANUELITA:
That's what it's called!

JOSELITO:
You're Daddy's little parrot. All you do is repeat.

MANUELITA:
No! Dad explained it!

JOSELITO:
Go look for some money. At the old gringo's desk

MANUELITA goes to the reception area and looks around.

MANUELITA:

I can't see anything.

JOSELITO:

Don't talk so loud, you idiot! They'll wake up.

MANUELITA:

I'm gonna tell Mom you called me an idiot.

JOSELITO:

Crybaby.

MANUELITA:

I am. I'm gonna tell her.

JOSELITO:

Come on, Manuelita. You're lucky I'm even including you in my plan. Here. Hold the phone.

MANUELITA does so. JOSELITO goes, suitcase and all, towards the reception area and looks for some money. He finally gives up. He sits on his suitcase.

JOSELITO:

Hang up the phone. We can't phone her.

MANUELITA does so. She goes and sits on JOSELITO's suitcase too. JUAN quietly descends the stairs, hoping to use the phone. He stops halfway when he sees MANUELITA and JOSELITO. He listens to the rest of the scene. The children don't know he's there.

MANUELITA:

Now what are we going to do?

JOSELITO:

I don't know. Can't you see I'm thinking?

MANUELITA:

Oh.

JOSELITO:

We never should have come with them. We should have just stayed with Grandma.

MANUELITA:
You think so?

JOSELITO:
They're crazy.

MANUELITA:
Really?

JOSELITO:
They're crazy and they're communists.

MANUELITA:
I don't think they're crazy. They were in jail, that's all.

JOSELITO:
Why do you think they were in jail?

MANUELITA:
'Cause.

JOSELITO:
'Cause why?

MANUELITA:
'Cause of the coup.

JOSELITO:
'Cause they're communists. Criminals. Bad people. Get it?

MANUELITA:
They're not bad people.

JOSELITO:
Yes, they are. Good people don't leave their kids behind just like
that. With no word.

MANUELITA:
They couldn't get us word 'cause they were political prisoners
and they weren't allowed to—

JOSELITO:
First of all, if they were good people they wouldn't just run off
and do bad things while they have children to raise. They
wouldn't have ended up in jail and got beaten up and stuff if
they were good—

MANUELITA:

It's not their fault that Chile was taken over by the military—

JOSELITO:

Yes it is! If they just minded their own business then none of this would have happened and we wouldn't have been left alone with Grandma for all those months and now we wouldn't be here with even more crazy people.

Pause.

MANUELITA:

Wasn't that weird to see Mom on the plane with those handcuffs?

JOSELITO:

Yeah.

MANUELITA:

And she looks so different.

JOSELITO:

Skinny.

MANUELITA:

And her nipples were cut off.

JOSELITO:

She's makin' that up.

MANUELITA:

No. I saw it.

JOSELITO:

Liar.

MANUELITA:

Just 'cause you don't wanna look doesn't mean they're liars.

Pause.

MANUELITA:

All these military guys raped her—

JOSELITO:

Shut up.

MANUELITA:
  Okay.

  Pause.

JOSELITO:
  They had her handcuffed to the airplane seat 'cause she's bad.

MANUELITA:
  Really?

JOSELITO:
  Yes. Really.

  *Both of them just stare ahead. JUAN remains. The rain
  continues to pour.*

Scene Six

*The next morning. CALLADITA and the RECEPTIONIST
are in the lobby of the hotel with the vacuum cleaner. The
RECEPTIONIST is teaching CALLADITA how to use it.*

RECEPTIONIST:
That's it. Press here. This button here. (*CALLADITA does so.*)
Presto.

RECEPTIONIST:
Now look. You pick up the hose here and you move it around
the floor like so. See? Now you try it.

*CALLADITA does so. At first she almost sucks up her own
dress into the vacuum. After some practice, she starts to get it.
She enjoys herself.*

RECEPTIONIST:
Atta girl. Quick learner.

CALLADITA keeps vacuuming.

RECEPTIONIST:
Hey! (*turning off the vacuum*) Maybe the next time that social
worker comes around I can tell her that you can take the
cleaning lady's place here. The lady quit after you guys got here,
but I wouldn't take it personally. You'll take her place and that
social worker won't have to find you a job. Whaddya think?

CALLADITA smiles and nods.

RECEPTIONIST:
Good. I'm just going to pop out and buy a newspaper. (*He starts
to leave, then turns around just before going off-stage.*) My name is
Jackie.

He leaves. CALLADITA vacuums for a few moments. She goes to the phone and picks it up. The sound of the dial tone fills the theatre. JUAN descends the stairs.

JUAN:
Are you on the phone?

CALLADITA jumps back, startled by JUAN's presence.

JUAN:
Oh, I didn't mean to scare you.

CALLADITA continues to stand there, the phone in her hand.

JUAN:
Are you on the phone?

CALLADITA shakes her head no.

JUAN:
Oh.

CALLADITA still stands there, the phone in her hand.

JUAN:
When you're done, let me know.

CALLADITA hands him the receiver.

JUAN:
Oh. Thank you. I figured out the times. I can phone La Chueca now. Wait till I tell her I escaped and came to Canada! Ha! My baby is going to die when I tell her I'm bringing her here! How do you use this thing?

CALLADITA points at the slots for coins.

JUAN:
Shit. Shoulda known. You have to pay for everything here, eh?

CALLADITA nods. The RECEPTIONIST enters with his newspaper.

JUAN:
I need to call Chile. I need to call my girlfriend in Chile!

RECEPTIONIST:
What's the number? Show me the number.

*CALLADITA leads JUAN to the reception desk and points at
the pad that the RECEPTIONIST is holding out.*

JUAN:
This is the number.

*The RECEPTIONIST hangs up the public phone and pulls
out a phone from behind his counter.*

RECEPTIONIST:
(*dialing*) Operator? Long distance call to Chile, please ... 238709
... (*passing the phone to JUAN*) There you go. It's ringing.

JUAN:
Oh my God. Hello? Is this La Huahua's Deli? Yes, is Miss
Natalia Sandoval there? I'm calling long distance; please let her
come to the phone. Please. Thank you ... Hello, Chueca? Baby,
you better sit down. What do you mean who's this? It's Juan!
Yes, Juan! I'm calling you from Canada! Yes! Canada! No, I'm
not joking! I ran away from the jail and I ended up on a
Swedish ship and now I'm in Canada! Of course I haven't lost
my marbles! No, Chuequita, this is totally legit. I'm going to
write you a long letter explaining everything, but right now I
want you to know that I'm bringing you here. That's right. I'm
bringing you here very, very soon ... What do you mean you
can't? ... No. Tell me now. No. Tell me right now. Chueca, I've
been sitting in jail for months thinking about you and then
sitting in a ship for weeks thinking about you, and now I finally
have you here on the phone. Don't disrespect me. Tell me now.
Now ... Chueca, the truth never hurts. Just tell me the brutal
truth. Don't lie ... What? No. No. No ... No, Chuequita, don't go.
No, Chuequita, I can forgive you anything. No. Don't go.
Chuequita. Don't.

*JUAN stands with the receiver in his hand. The sound of
Chueca hanging up the phone. Static. A dial tone. The
RECEPTIONIST takes the phone from JUAN, listens to the
dial tone and hangs up. JUAN stands in a total daze.*

JUAN:
This can't be happening.

*CALLADITA motions to the RECEPTIONIST to do his own
thing. The RECEPTIONIST pretends to read the newspaper.
CALLADITA takes JUAN to the couch.*

JUAN:
This can't be happening. Nope. Nope. Nope. This isn't
happening. This can't be true.
    She shacked up with my lazy brother. He stands on the
street corner all day with his buddies whistling at the girls. She
was doing my brother the whole time she was standing in line
at the jail bringing me empanadas. My brother.
    Oh, God. Here it comes. The pain. Here it comes. Oh, shit.

CALLADITA:
Rock. Like this.

RECEPTIONIST:
She talked.

*CALLADITA and JUAN rock. FAT JORGE and CONDOR
PASSES descend the stairs.*

FAT JORGE:
Alright, boys. Time to go on our job search. (*seeing JUAN and
CALLADITA rocking*) What are you two doing?

CALLADITA:
Just rocking. That's all.

FAT JORGE:
Oh. Juan—She talked! SHE TALKED! CALLADITA TALKED!

*MANUELITA, JOSELITO, FLACA, and CAKEHEAD come
barrelling down the stairs.*

FLACA:
She talked?!

CALLADITA nods.

FLACA:
Oh my God! Talk again! Talk again!

CALLADITA:
Hello, my name is Isabel Paez de la Rosa.

Everyone gathers around her and hugs her, squealing.

JUAN:
You sounded so natural when you talked that I totally forgot you're mute!

FAT JORGE:
Let's have a toast!

FLACA:
No! Fat Jorge, you can't get drunk all the time!

FAT JORGE:
Who said anything about getting drunk?

FLACA:
No. You guys go on your job search—

MANUELITA:
Uncle Juan, are you okay?

JUAN:
Why do you ask?

JOSELITO:
Oh, no. He looks like he's gonna start cryin'. Just like everybody else.

JUAN:
No. I'm not going to start crying.

CAKEHEAD:
If you wanna cry, comrade, cry for fuck's sake.

JUAN:
I said no. I will not cry.

JOSELITO:
Good.

FLACA:
Go on your job search! Go!

The men exit.

Scene Seven

FLACA and CAKEHEAD hug CALLADITA. PAT and BILL enter.

BILL:
Comrades. Pat, good news.

FLACA:
Good news?

BILL:
Very much good news.

CAKEHEAD:
Tell us what the good news is already.

CALLADITA:
Yeah!

BILL:
Okay—Oh, God me. (*to CALLADITA*) You speak.

CAKEHEAD:
Yes! Now tell us what the good news is!

BILL:
Okay. We find job at Fat Jorge. Steel mill. Work all night. Maintenance work. Job at you, Flaca, fish cannery, work all day. We find you home. Projects in Strathcona. That Chinatown.

FLACA:
Okay, okay. When do we start?

PAT:
Have you told them about the school for the kids?

BILL:

Oh, yeah. We find school for kids. In Strathcona too. You move tomorrow.

FLACA:

Tomorrow?

BILL:

Yeah. Interfaith Church donate furniture, bed, table, and chairs, things more. You and Fat Jorge work next week.

FLACA:

Sounds good. Very good. Thank you. Thank you very much.

BILL:

Cakehead. Work all night on a bakery. Bake bread.

CAKEHEAD:

Okay. Okay. I can bake bread. Sure. I can do that.

BILL:

And you and Calladita live on top Condor Passes and Juan. In projects also—

PAT:

Tell them about the other jobs—

RECEPTIONIST:

Wait a minute. You got them jobs?

PAT:

Yes—

RECEPTIONIST:

Because Kaladeeda has a job. I told her she could be the new cleaning lady here.

PAT:

Really?

RECEPTIONIST:

Yup. She's hired.

BILL:

(*to CALLADITA*) You work here as cleaning lady?

CALLADITA:
I am? That's great!

PAT:
Well, that's settled. Okay, have you told them about Manuel?

BILL:
You mean Condor Passes?

PAT:
Uh—

BILL:
Condor Passes—incidentally, where is the men?

JOSELITO:
On a job search.

BILL:
Shit. Why lose time in that? Nobody give them job that way. Okay. Job for Condor Passes. Gardener at UBC garden botanical. Father of Pat member of Forestry School and get Condor job—

CAKEHEAD:
Excellent. Excellent.

BILL:
And Juan: two paper routes and cleaning a daycare—

The men enter. JUAN is wearing a chicken costume.

FAT JORGE:
Comrade Bill! Our respected social worker! Please! Make yourselves at home! Have we got news for you! (*pointing to JUAN in the chicken costume*) This one is literally fresh off the boat and look at him! We got here before him and he's the one that gets a job! Son of a bitch.

JOSELITO:
Is that Uncle Juan in there?

JUAN:
Yes! It's me! Look, you can see my face through the beak!

JOSELITO:
I wanna wear one of those!

MANUELITA:
Me too!

JOSELITO:
Copycat.

MANUELITA:
Show off!

PAT:
What's going on?

BILL:
It would seem that Juan already got a job that involves wearing that degrading costume.

FAT JORGE:
So he's like literally fresh off the boat and we walk by this fried chicken place and Juan goes in there and says, "Me job," and before you know it they've got him in this chicken costume and all he has to do is dance cumbia on the corner there.

BILL:
Juan, you not do that job: (*enunciating every syllable*) Humiliation—

JUAN:
Are you kidding? Getting paid to dance on a corner all day? I gotta go back. My new boss will think I stole the uniform.

JUAN exits.

BILL:
Uniform?

FLACA:
(*to FAT JORGE and CONDOR PASSES*) We're all getting out of here tomorrow. They've found us all homes and jobs. We're leaving the refugee hotel.

Everyone looks at each other, in silence. They look around the hotel.

Scene Eight

Later that night. FAT JORGE and FLACA are in the middle of a confrontation in the lobby. FAT JORGE drinks. The remainder of the cast witnesses it from different spots on the stairs and the lobby.

FAT JORGE:
Don't look at me like that.

FLACA:
Like what?

FAT JORGE:
Like I'm the only bad guy here. Like you're not a traitor too.

FLACA:
(*trying to take the bottle from him*) Fat Jorge, you've gotta stop drinking—

FAT JORGE:
You betrayed me. And the kids.

FLACA:
I took an oath.

FAT JORGE:
You also took an oath with me.

FLACA:
I tried to keep you guys as well, because I couldn't choose. Maybe that was my mistake—

FAT JORGE:
I would have joined too if you'd told me to.

FLACA:
No. I thought about it. And now I see I was correct in not telling you. You don't have what it takes—

FAT JORGE:
(*throwing the bottle on the floor, where it smashes to smithereens*)
No! I'm not the crème de la crème!

BILL O'NEILL, with JUAN's help, takes the children away from their parents, off-stage. FLACA goes to her room. FAT JORGE stays in the lobby. CALLADITA starts to clean up the glass.

Scene Nine

Later that night. CAKEHEAD knocks on CONDOR
PASSES's door. She is holding a cake she just baked. It has
one candle on it. CONDOR PASSES opens the door.

CAKEHEAD:
(*in a whisper so as not to disturb the sleeping hotel*) Happy birthday
to you, happy birthday to you—

CONDOR PASSES:
Cakehead—What the—

CAKEHEAD:
—Shhhh!—Happy birthday, dear Condor—

CONDOR PASSES:
How did—

CAKEHEAD:
Shut up—Happy birthday to you!

CONDOR PASSES:
I just don't—

CAKEHEAD:
Blow!

CONDOR PASSES:
Huh?

CAKEHEAD:
Blow! The candle!

CONDOR PASSES:
Oh.

Pause as CAKEHEAD and CONDOR PASSES stare at each other awkwardly.

CAKEHEAD:

Holy fucking Jesus. Are you gonna blow the candle or do I have to slap you now?

CONDOR PASSES blows out the candle.

CAKEHEAD:

Spit all over me now too, why dontcha.

CONDOR PASSES:
Oh, sorry.

CAKEHEAD:
So? Can I come in?

CONDOR PASSES:
Uh, yeah, yeah. Of course. It's a bit—

CAKEHEAD:
Messy? I can see that.

CAKEHEAD makes her way to the kitchenette and starts to cut the cake, arranging two slices on plates.

CONDOR PASSES:
What time is it?

CAKEHEAD:
Around 12:05.

Another big awkward pause as CAKEHEAD approaches CONDOR PASSES with his slice. They arrange themselves on the floor, after looking awkwardly at the bed. They begin to eat.

CONDOR PASSES:
This is very good.

CAKEHEAD:
You can make them from packages here.

CONDOR PASSES:
Packages?

CAKEHEAD:

I went to the supermarket up the street and I found a whole section of different kinds of packages for cakes. You just add water and eggs and that's all. Are you eating?

CONDOR PASSES:

Yeah.

Long awkward pause as they both eat.

CAKEHEAD:

I wonder where we'll be living.

CONDOR PASSES:

I don't know. But I'll be a gardener.

CAKEHEAD:

And I'll be a baker. Have you ever gardened before?

CONDOR PASSES:

No. I worked the assembly line at the RCA Victor factory. And I worked for the union. Night and day. Have you ever baked?

CAKEHEAD:

Just the pottery. I make beautiful pottery, you know.

CONDOR PASSES:

What does it look like?

CAKEHEAD:

Big bowls shaped like salmon and seashells and the craters on the moon.

CONDOR PASSES:

You worked with your hands. And so did I.

CAKEHEAD:

And we will still work with our hands. I'll knead dough and you'll dig up the earth.

Pause as they continue to eat and look at each other awkwardly.

CAKEHEAD:

So. You're eighteen now. A man.

CONDOR PASSES:
    How did you know?

CAKEHEAD:
    Looked at your passport.

CONDOR PASSES:
    You looked at my passport?

CAKEHEAD:
    I looked at your passport.

CONDOR PASSES:
    You looked at my passport?

CAKEHEAD:
    Yes, I told you that already.

CONDOR PASSES:
    When did—

CAKEHEAD:
    I came into your room the other day and I saw your passport
    lying on the bed here and I looked at it—

CONDOR PASSES:
    Why were you in my room?

CAKEHEAD:
    I wanted to smell it.

CONDOR PASSES:
    Oh.

CAKEHEAD:
    I wanted to smell your room and I saw the passport on the bed
    and I just couldn't help myself.

CONDOR PASSES:
    How did it smell?

CAKEHEAD:
    The passport?

CONDOR PASSES:
    No. The room.

CAKEHEAD:

Good. Good. Like home. Your poncho, your sheets, the armpit of your shirt, it all smells like the house where I was born, with the kelp and the seaweed drying on the sill ... You smell like our roots, you smell so good, so good, so good, I could burst from the smell of it all, from the smell of you and your pain and the look in your eyes—

CONDOR PASSES moves closer to her. He positions himself very close to her. She leans over and smells his hair, his skin, his breath, his clothes. He surrenders to her.

CAKEHEAD:

(*smelling in great big breaths*) Ohh! You smell like that floor. Just waxed. And the mud on the road after a fresh rain.

CAKEHEAD starts to unbutton CONDOR PASSES's shirt. He allows himself to be taken.

CAKEHEAD:

(*smelling his chest, neck, and underarms*) You smell like my past, the good past, the one that existed so long ago—

CONDOR PASSES:

I come from Santiago. The smell of diesel and peanuts cooking in caramel, the smell of open sewers and tear gas, suffocating me—

CAKEHEAD:

Am I suffocating you?

CONDOR PASSES:

No! I can breathe, I can breathe, I can breathe you in, but I can't smell. Nothing. I can smell nothing.

CAKEHEAD:

Breathe through your nose. (*offering her mouth*) Smell my breath.

CAKEHEAD:

Can you taste?

CONDOR PASSES:

No. Nothing.

CAKEHEAD:
  Can you feel?

CONDOR PASSES:
  I think so.

CAKEHEAD:
  You're shaking.

CONDOR PASSES:
  I've never done this before.

CAKEHEAD:
  Just keep breathing. Breathe like the seven volcanoes in the deep south of Chile.

CONDOR PASSES:
  I've never been with a woman before.

CAKEHEAD:
  Oh.

CONDOR PASSES:
  I'm afraid.

CAKEHEAD:
  Don't be.

CONDOR PASSES:
  Wait. There's something I have to tell you. I can't feel down there. I'm numb there. I wasn't born like that. They did it to me.

CAKEHEAD:
  Does it hurt?

CONDOR PASSES:
  Nothing hurts anymore.

CAKEHEAD:
  Let me love you. Let me worship you. You shine like copper and I could kiss you forever.

CONDOR PASSES:
  Kiss me forever. Kiss me forever ...

The CUECA DANCER emerges and does his zapateo as "La Partida" by Inti-Illimani begins to play. They embrace and eventually make love, on the floor. As CONDOR PASSES and CAKEHEAD make love, FAT JORGE goes up to the room to join FLACA. JUAN, who is with MANUELITA and JOSELITO in his room, makes his way to the lobby, where CALLADITA is rocking in a fetal position on the couch. JOSELITO and MANUELITA stay in JUAN's room. JUAN approaches CALLADITA and lies next to her, spooning her. He rocks too. FAT JORGE tries to make love to FLACA in their room. She pushes him away and locks herself in the bathroom. FAT JORGE collapses on the bed. MANUELITA and JOSELITO make shadows with their hands on the wall of JUAN's room.

Scene Ten

CALLADITA and JUAN OF THE CHICKENS are asleep,
curled up on the couch in the lobby. JOSELITO and
MANUELITA have fallen asleep in JUAN's room. CONDOR
PASSES and CAKEHEAD are asleep on CONDOR's bed.
FAT JORGE is asleep on his bed. FLACA looks out the
window of their room, smoking a cigarette.

FAT JORGE's nightmare returns to haunt him. He takes on
his usual shape, as do FLACA and MANUEL. The rest of the
cast contribute to the soundscape. FAT JORGE sees something
terrible directly in front of him.

WOMAN (played by FLACA):
Don't let them take my baby! They're going to sell her to a
military family! That's what they're doing! Stealing babies!

She screams. FAT JORGE screams.

FLACA:
(shaking him awake) Fat Jorge! Fat Jorge!

FAT JORGE:
Oh, shit. Oh, shit.

FLACA:
It's the nightmare again.

FAT JORGE:
I have to puke.

FLACA:
It's okay, my little big bear. It's okay.

FLACA holds him. He finally cries. And cries. And cries.

FAT JORGE:
Please don't go. Please don't leave me. Please.

Scene Eleven

The next morning. It rains like hell. MANUELITA and JOSELITO contemplate the RECEPTIONIST as he dusts the lava lamp. All the adults are in their rooms, packing their bags. The RECEPTIONIST whistles "Somewhere Over the Rainbow." PAT and BILL enter.

PAT:
Hi, kids!

JOSELITO and MANUELITA:
Hola!

JOSELITO:
Bill O'Neill!

The adults start to descend the stairs with their bags.

FAT JORGE:
I do believe that I will never see the sun again in this fucking country.

BILL:
You will, you will. In three months more.

FAT JORGE:
Three more months?!

BILL:
Okay. Four maybe.

FAT JORGE:
Christ.

CAKEHEAD:
It's like Mapuche land. It really is.

PAT:

(*opening her bag and pulling out gifts, talking to MANUELITA and JOSELITO*) I've brought you some gifts. Just small little toys, but I really wanted to express to you two just how brave you are and how good you are and how much you remind me of myself when I was a small child and we first arrived in this country. (*choking up*) And that even though I don't speak your language, I want to be considered your auntie too. And, Bill, don't translate that. They're kids. They understand the heart of what I just said.

PAT gives the kids their gifts. She hugs them tightly.

PAT:

Well, the volunteers should be arriving any minute now to take you to your new homes. Bill, translation please.

BILL:

Interfaith Church come in van, me got station wagon, and couple of my friends coming in VW van too. They good gringos. Run away from California because not go war in Vietnam. They solidarity.

MANUELITA:

Where are we going to live, Mommy?

FLACA:

I don't know. I'm sure it'll be nice.

FAT JORGE:

And you'll be going to school tomorrow, kids. Brand new school for you.

JOSELITO:

Will I make friends there?

FLACA:

I'm sure you will, Joselito. I'm sure you will.

JOSELITO:

I hope so.

FAT JORGE:
I can't believe Juan of the Chickens. Within a few days of his arrival he's got a job and a girlfriend.

CAKEHEAD:
And he made her talk.

CALLADITA:
He's got a way about him, my Juan.

BILL:
You two now lovers?

CAKEHEAD:
Yeah, Juan of the Chickens and Calladita and me and Condor Passes.

BILL:
You chilis act with velocity.

CAKEHEAD:
That's right, brother. We work fast. No time for in-between. Either you're in or you're out. Either you're hot or you're cold. Either you're on the left or on the right. Remember: we come from a land of active volcanoes, massive earthquakes, the highest mountains in the Americas, the driest desert in the world, a huge hunk of ice to the south and the violent Pacific to the west.

CALLADITA:
By the way, Bill. Me and Juan of the Chickens are going to take the place you had gotten for Cakehead and me. Cakehead and Condor Passes will take the one meant for the men.

BILL:
Okay. (to PAT) Pat, this may come as a shock to you, but it seems that things have gotten hot and heavy here at the refugee hotel in the last couple of nights—

PAT:
Oh please, Bill. I'm not blind. Same thing happened with us Hungarians when we first arrived. Here are the volunteers.

BILL:

Okay, you very velocity chilis. Off we go.

FAT JORGE:

Off we go.

FLACA:

Come on, kids. Say goodbye to the old gringo.

All the Chileans pile around the counter and hug and kiss the RECEPTIONIST goodbye. They thank him profusely.

RECEPTIONIST:

(*handing the record player to FAT JORGE*) I want you to have this. So you can listen to your record.

BILL:

(*to FAT JORGE*) Gift to you.

FAT JORGE:

Oh my God. Thank you, esteemed old gringo. Thank you.

FAT JORGE embraces the RECEPTIONIST.

RECEPTIONIST:

De nada. (*taking a camera from his desk*) I would like to photograph you before you go.

JOSELITO:

He wants to take a picture!

BILL:

Right now, everybody, stand there! All you!

FAT JORGE:

(*to BILL and PAT*) Come and join us!

BILL:

No. This picture of you.

The RECEPTIONIST takes the picture. This is a suspended moment, with a loud sound effect of a shutter.

Epilogue

The entire cast remains frozen in the photograph position.
MANUELITA breaks away from the photo and refers to each
one of the characters as she speaks, thirty years later.

ADULT MANUELITA:
Juan of the Chickens ended up forming a union of all the
people in his field: sandwich-board people, sports mascots,
singing telegram workers. He now leads the union, which has
gone national. Flaca, my mom, worked at the cannery for many
years. She put herself through school again, revalidated her
degree and she's now one of the top professors in pedagogy at
SFU. Fat Jorge, my dad, worked at the steel mill for a decade.
He drank and drank and drank. My mother eventually left him
for Bill O'Neill, and my dad drank himself to death on skid row.
He lived in the open wound and he died in the open wound.
My brother Joselito, always the rebel, became a stock broker.
Cakehead baked bread for many years. She put her potter skills
to good use with the dough. She now owns the most successful
bakery in East Vancouver. It's called Cakehead's Delicacies. She
specializes in gingerbread houses depicting real-life
experiences, such as people attempting suicide by sticking their
heads in electric ovens or jumping off the third floor of a
building only to land in a dumpster of fibreglass. Calladita is
head of housekeeping at the refugee hotel, and, yes, she's still
with Juan of the Chickens. Condor Passes died of a brain
aneurysm while lying in Cakehead's arms. All those blows to
the head finally caught up to him. They had just made love.
And nine months later Cakehead gave birth to a beautiful baby
boy. No one knows how it happened—but Cakehead said that
Mapungenechen, the Great Mother, had her hand in it.

Cakehead named the baby Salvador, after Allende. Pat Kelemen keeps in touch; she's one of Cakehead's regular gingerbread clients. As for me, I just do what my dad told me to do when I was a little girl: I keep my eyes and ears open. Oh, yeah. The receptionist filled a wall with photographs, because many, many, many more refugees came to stay at the refugee hotel. From Guatemala, El Salvador, Vietnam, Iran, Ethiopia, Somalia, Yugoslavia, Colombia, Iraq ...

The CUECA DANCER appears, doing his light zapateo.

ADULT MANUELITA:

It takes courage to remember, it takes courage to forget. It takes a hero to do both.

The end.

About the Playwright

CARMEN AGUIRRE is a Vancouver-based theatre artist who has worked extensively in North and South America. She has written and co-written twenty-one plays, including *Chile Con Carne, The Trigger, The Refugee Hotel,* and *Blue Box.* Her first non-fiction book, *Something Fierce: Memoirs of a Revolutionary Daughter,* was published in 2011 by Douglas & McIntyre in Canada and Granta/Portobello in the United Kingdom and is now available in Finland and Holland, in translation. *Something Fierce* was nominated for British Columbia's National Award for Canadian Non-Fiction, the international Charles Taylor Prize for Literary Non-Fiction, was a finalist for the 2012 Hubert Evans Non-Fiction Prize (BC Book Prizes), was selected by the *Globe and Mail, Quill & Quire,* and the *National Post* as one of the best books of 2011, was named Book of the Week by BBC Radio in the United Kingdom, won CBC Canada Reads 2012, and became a number-one national bestseller.

Aguirre has more than sixty film, TV, and stage acting credits. She is a Theatre of the Oppressed workshop facilitator and an instructor in the acting department at Vancouver Film School. She received the Union of B.C. Performers 2011 Lorena Gale Woman of Distinction Award, the 2012 Langara College Outstanding Alumnae Award, and has been nominated for a Jessie Richardson Theatre Award, a Dora Mavor Moore Award, and the prestigious Siminovitch Prize.

Aguirre is a graduate of Langara College's Studio 58.

Also by Carmen Aguirre

DRAMA

Blue Box *
Chile Con Carne
    (in the anthology *Rave: Young Adult Drama*)
¿QUE PASA with LA RAZA, eh?
    (in the anthology *Along Human Lines: Dramas from*
    Refugee Lives)
The Trigger *

NON-FICTION

Mexican Hooker #1 and My Other Roles Since the Revolution
Something Fierce: Memoirs of a Revolutionary Daughter

* Published by Talonbooks